WELCOME TO THE U.S.A.

WYOMING

Written by Ann Heinrichs   Illustrated by Matt Kania
Content Adviser: Ellen Stump, Historian, Wyoming
State Historic Preservation Office, Cheyenne, Wyoming

The Child's World

Published in the United States of America by The Child's World®
PO Box 326 • Chanhassen, MN 55317-0326
800-599-READ • www.childsworld.com

Photo Credits

Cover: Getty Images/Digital Vision; frontispiece: Swift/Vanuga Images/Corbis.

Interior: AP/Wide World Photo: 6 (Kevork Djansezian), 13 (The Jackson Hole News); Connie Brewer/Celtic Festival and Highland Games: 30; Corbis: 9 (Jan Butchofsky-Houser), 10 (Swift/Vanuga Images), 14 (James L. Amos), 21 (Jonathan Blair), 25 (Owen Franken), 26 (Bill Ross), 34 (Phil Schermeister); Getty Images/Robert Nickelsberg: 18; Library of Congress: 16; Buddy Mays/Corbis: 17, 22; Star Valley Cheese Company: 29; Wyoming Dinosaur Center: 33.

Acknowledgments

The Child's World®: Mary Berendes, Publishing Director

Editorial Directions, Inc.: E. Russell Primm, Editorial Director; Katie Marsico, Associate Editor; Judith Shiffer, Assistant Editor; Matt Messbarger, Editorial Assistant; Susan Hindman, Copy Editor; Melissa McDaniel, Proofreader; Kevin Cunningham, Peter Garnham, Matt Messbarger, Olivia Nellums, Chris Simms, Molly Symmonds, Katherine Trickle, Carl Stephen Wender, Fact Checkers; Tim Griffin/IndexServ, Indexer; Cian Loughlin O'Day, Photo Researcher and Editor

The Design Lab: Kathleen Petelinsek, Design; Julia Goozen, Art Production

Library of Congress Cataloging-in-Publication Data

Heinrichs, Ann.
  Wyoming / by Ann Heinrichs ; cartography and illustrations by Matt Kania.
    p. cm. — (Welcome to the U.S.A.)
  Includes index.
  ISBN 1-59296-491-5 (library bound : alk. paper)
  1. Wyoming—Juvenile literature. I. Kania, Matt, ill. II. Title.
F761.3.H456 2006
978.7—dc22   2005014808

Ann Heinrichs is the author of more than 100 books for children and young adults. She has also enjoyed successful careers as a children's book editor and an advertising copywriter. Ann grew up in Fort Smith, Arkansas, and lives in Chicago, Illinois.

About the Author
Ann Heinrichs

Matt Kania loves maps and, as a kid, dreamed of making them. In school he studied geography and cartography, and today he makes maps for a living. Matt's favorite thing about drawing maps is learning about the places they represent. Many of the maps he has created can be found in books, magazines, videos, Web sites, and public places.

About the
Map Illustrator
Matt Kania

On the cover: Check out the Upper Geyser Basin at Yellowstone National Park!
On page one: The Shoshone Indian tribe calls Wyoming home.

OUR WYOMING TRIP

You're in for a great trip through Wyoming! Just follow that dotted line. Or else skip around. Either way, you're in for lots of fun!

You'll hang out with cowboys and mountain men. You'll see where famous outlaws hid. You'll watch water spewing into the air. You'll pan for gold and stay on a ranch. And you'll dig for dinosaur bones!

There's plenty more to do in Wyoming. So buckle up and let's hit the road!

WELCOME TO WYOMING

As you travel through Wyoming, watch for all the interesting facts along the way.

4

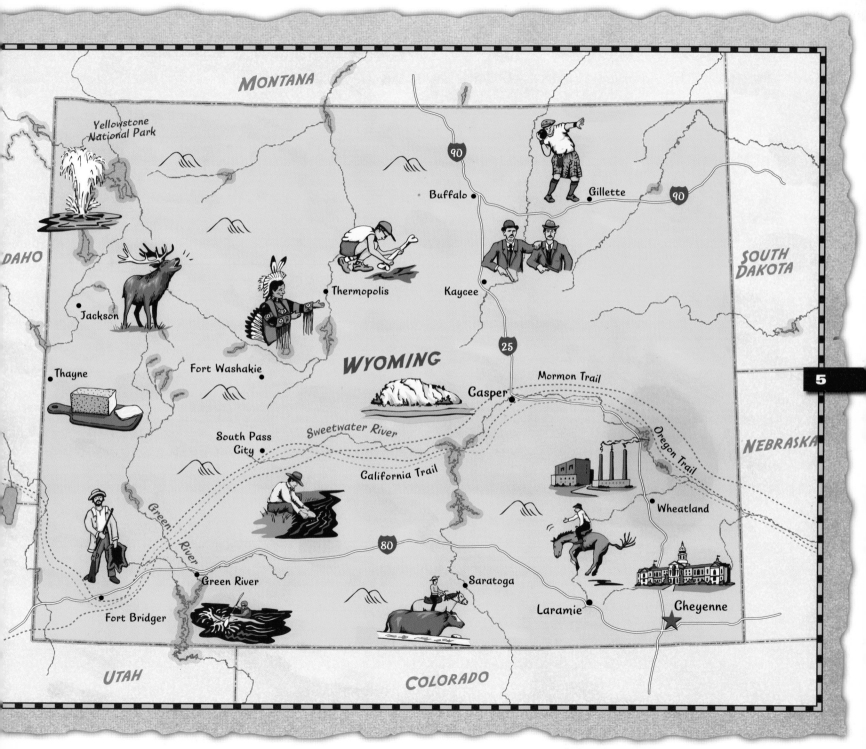

MONTANA

Yellowstone
National Park

IDAHO

Jackson

Thayne

Fort Washakie

Thermopolis

Buffalo

Kaycee

Gillette

90

90

SOUTH
DAKOTA

5

WYOMING

Casper

Mormon Trail

25

Sweetwater River

South Pass
City

California Trail

Oregon Trail

NEBRASKA

Green River

Wheatland

80

Green River

Saratoga

Laramie

Cheyenne

Fort Bridger

UTAH

COLORADO

The Black Hills rise in northeastern Wyoming. They continue into South Dakota.

Yeow! That water is hot! Geysers are just some of Yellowstone's natural wonders.

Yellowstone's main entrances in Wyoming are Jackson and Cody.

Yellowstone National Park

Bubbling **mudpots** are belching out gases. **Geysers** are spewing super-hot water high into the air. You're at Yellowstone National Park! This area was a fantastic sight for explorers. And it's just as fantastic today for tourists.

Yellowstone is in Wyoming's Rocky Mountain Region. The Rockies run through much of the state. They're broken into several mountain ranges. The beautiful Teton Range is near Jackson. High, dry basins lie between the mountain ranges.

High plains cover eastern Wyoming. Thousands of cattle and sheep graze there.

Some rivers have carved out deep canyons. One such river is the Green River. It flows through western Wyoming.

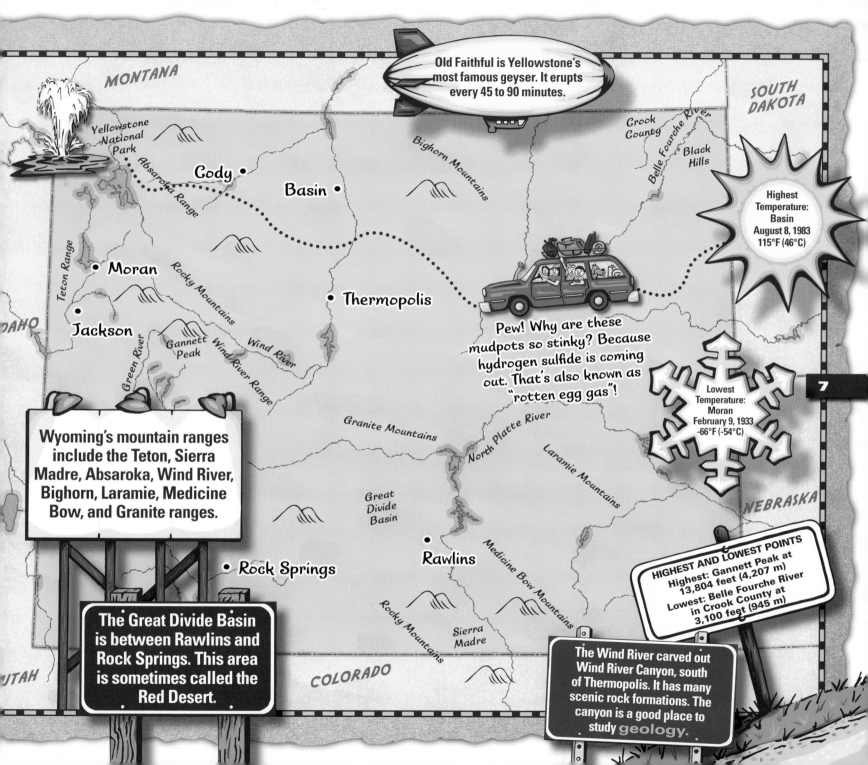

MONTANA

Old Faithful is Yellowstone's most famous geyser. It erupts every 45 to 90 minutes.

SOUTH DAKOTA

Yellowstone National Park

Absaroka Range

Cody •

Basin •

Bighorn Mountains

Crook County

Belle Fourche River

Black Hills

Highest Temperature: Basin August 8, 1983 115°F (46°C)

Teton Range

• Moran

Rocky Mountains

• Jackson

Gannett Peak

Green River

Wind River Range

Wind River

• Thermopolis

Pew! Why are these mudpots so stinky? Because hydrogen sulfide is coming out. That's also known as "rotten egg gas"!

IDAHO

7

Lowest Temperature: Moran February 9, 1933 -66°F (-54°C)

Granite Mountains

North Platte River

Laramie Mountains

NEBRASKA

Wyoming's mountain ranges include the Teton, Sierra Madre, Absaroka, Wind River, Bighorn, Laramie, Medicine Bow, and Granite ranges.

Great Divide Basin

• Rawlins

Medicine Bow Mountains

HIGHEST AND LOWEST POINTS
Highest: Gannett Peak at 13,804 feet (4,207 m)
Lowest: Belle Fourche River in Crook County at 3,100 feet (945 m)

• Rock Springs

The Great Divide Basin is between Rawlins and Rock Springs. This area is sometimes called the Red Desert.

UTAH

Rocky Mountains

Sierra Madre

COLORADO

The Wind River carved out Wind River Canyon, south of Thermopolis. It has many scenic rock formations. The canyon is a good place to study geology.

STATE TREE
PLAINS
COTTONWOOD

STATE BIRD
MEADOWLARK

STATE FLOWER
INDIAN
PAINTBRUSH

Let's take a sleigh ride through the elk refuge! We get on at the National Museum of Wildlife Art. It's in Jackson Hole, a valley near Jackson.

MONTANA

Grand Teton National Park

Jackson Hole

IDAHO

• Jackson

Rocky Mountains

SOUTH DAKOT

Mortenson Lake National Wildlife Refuge is southwest of Laramie. It's closed to visitors, though. The refuge protects the **endangered** Wyoming toad.

Rocky Mountains

UTAH

The National Park Service has 7 sites in Wyoming.

NEBRA

• Laramie

About 3,000 elk spend the summer in Grand Teton National Park. It's just north of Jackson.

COLORADO

The National Elk Refuge

Thousands of elk move across the snowy ground. They look like big, shaggy deer. You're visiting the National Elk Refuge! It's north of Jackson. More than 7,500 elk spend the winter here.

Elk are some of Wyoming's largest animals. Grizzly bears and moose are big ones, too. You'll see mountain sheep high in the Rockies. Mountain lions also lurk in the mountains. Deer and antelope graze on the plains.

Wyoming also has lots of smaller animals. There are beavers, raccoons, ferrets, foxes, and rabbits. Trappers used to hunt some of them. Then they sold the furry skins.

These elk spend winter in the National Elk Refuge.

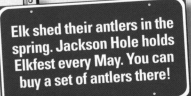

Elk shed their antlers in the spring. Jackson Hole holds Elkfest every May. You can buy a set of antlers there!

This Shoshone girl wears traditional dress. She's attending Eastern Shoshone Indian Days.

Eastern Shoshone Indian Days

Want to learn about Native American **culture**? Then attend Eastern Shoshone Indian Days in Fort Washakie. It's on the Wind River Indian **Reservation.**

Powwows are Native American gatherings. Indians come from far away to take part. They wear **traditional** dress. And they compete in dancing and drumming contests.

Many Indian groups once lived in Wyoming. Most groups hunted bison across the plains. Bison provided more than meat. Horns and hoofs made everything from tools to toys. Hides were used for clothes and blankets.

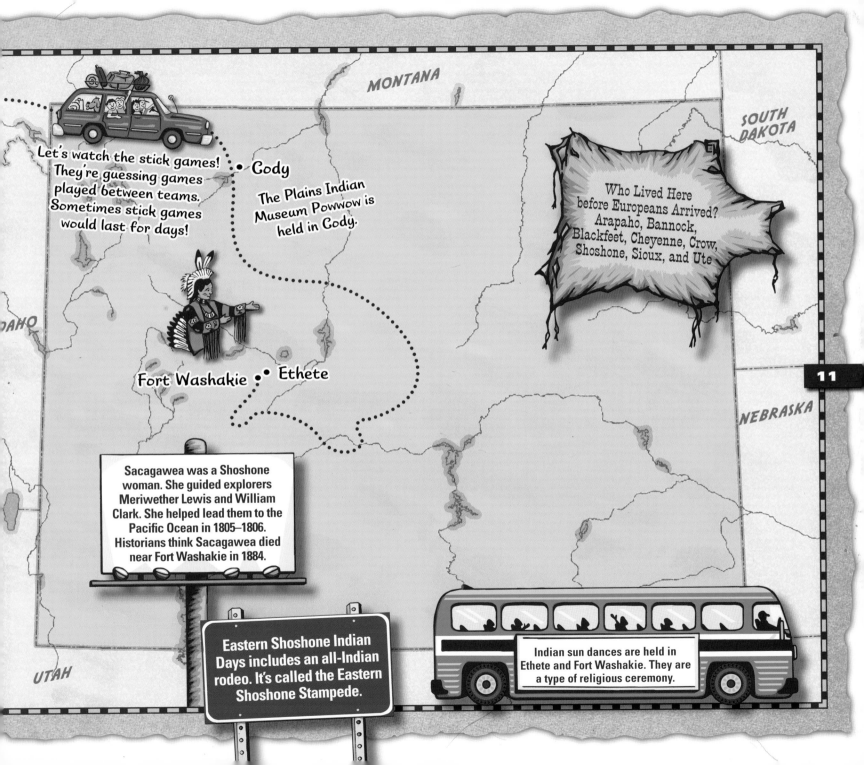

Let's watch the stick games! They're guessing games played between teams. Sometimes stick games would last for days!

Cody
The Plains Indian Museum Powwow is held in Cody.

MONTANA

SOUTH DAKOTA

Who Lived Here before Europeans Arrived? Arapaho, Bannock, Blackfeet, Cheyenne, Crow, Shoshone, Sioux, and Ute

IDAHO

Fort Washakie • Ethete

NEBRASKA

Sacagawea was a Shoshone woman. She guided explorers Meriwether Lewis and William Clark. She helped lead them to the Pacific Ocean in 1805–1806. Historians think Sacagawea died near Fort Washakie in 1884.

Eastern Shoshone Indian Days includes an all-Indian rodeo. It's called the Eastern Shoshone Stampede.

Indian sun dances are held in Ethete and Fort Washakie. They are a type of religious ceremony.

UTAH

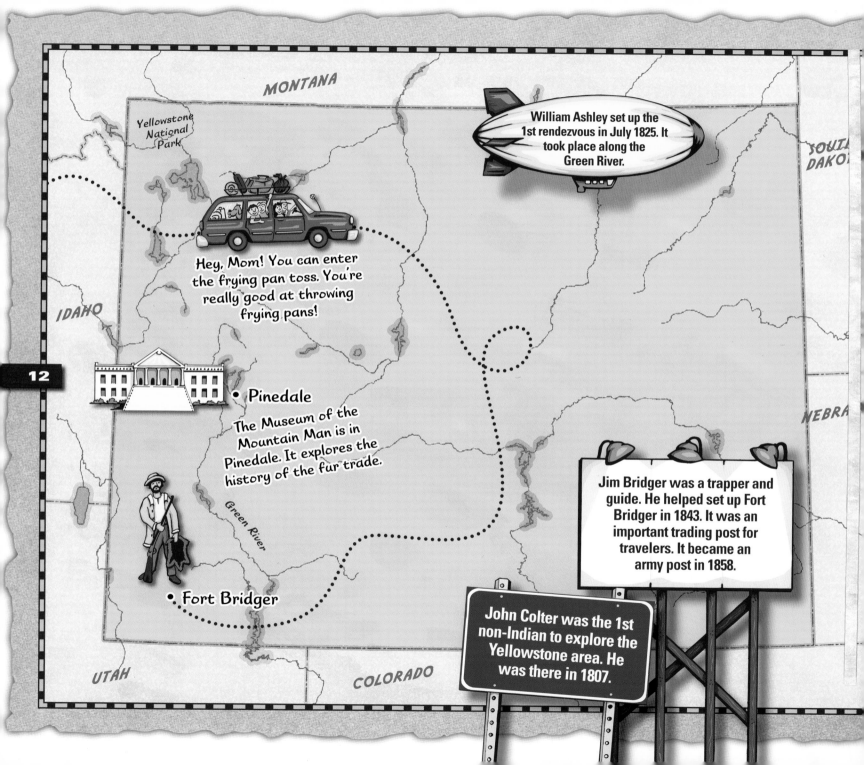

MONTANA

Yellowstone
National
Park

IDAHO

UTAH

COLORADO

SOUTH DAKOTA

NEBRASKA

William Ashley set up the
1st rendezvous in July 1825. It
took place along the
Green River.

Hey, Mom! You can enter
the frying pan toss. You're
really good at throwing
frying pans!

• Pinedale

The Museum of the
Mountain Man is in
Pinedale. It explores the
history of the fur trade.

Green River

• Fort Bridger

Jim Bridger was a trapper and
guide. He helped set up Fort
Bridger in 1843. It was an
important trading post for
travelers. It became an
army post in 1858.

John Colter was the 1st
non-Indian to explore the
Yellowstone area. He
was there in 1807.

Fort Bridger's Mountain Man Rendezvous

Watch the bow-and-arrow contest. See how mountain men started campfires without matches. Or check out the kids' games. Indian drummers and dancers are performing. And tents and tepees surround the camp. It's Fort Bridger's Mountain Man **Rendezvous**!

Wyoming was once part of France's Louisiana Territory. The United States bought this region in 1803. Then explorers and fur trappers came into Wyoming.

Fur trappers met at a rendezvous every summer. Their Indian friends joined them, too. They traded furs for supplies. They told stories and played games. It was a great party!

Wonder what life was like on the frontier? Find out at Fort Bridger's Mountain Man Rendezvous.

Want to travel back in time? Just stop by South Pass City. You'll think you did.

The National Historic Trails Interpretive Center is in Casper. It highlights various cross-country trails and the pioneers who traveled them.

Gold Rush Days in South Pass City

Try bowling with a tiny ball. Kids in the 1800s played this game. Or try panning for gold in the creek. It's time for Gold Rush Days! It's at South Pass City State Historic Site.

Many pioneers began heading west in the 1840s. Their trails went through South Pass. It was a well-known passage through the mountains.

Gold was discovered in Wyoming in 1867. It was in the mountains west of South Pass. Thousands of eager gold miners swarmed into town. Gold lured miners through northern and eastern Wyoming, too. The miners tore through Indian lands. Indians fought to keep their land. But U.S. soldiers finally defeated them.

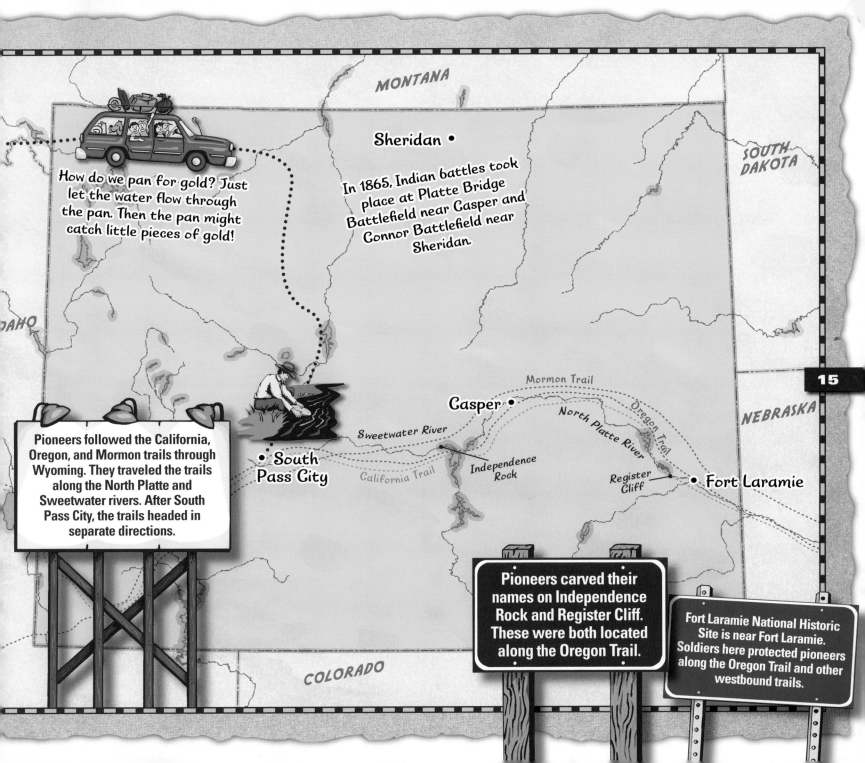

MONTANA

Sheridan •

How do we pan for gold? Just let the water flow through the pan. Then the pan might catch little pieces of gold!

In 1865, Indian battles took place at Platte Bridge Battlefield near Casper and Connor Battlefield near Sheridan.

SOUTH DAKOTA

IDAHO

NEBRASKA

Mormon Trail

Casper •

Oregon Trail

Sweetwater River

North Platte River

• South Pass City

Independence Rock

California Trail

Register Cliff

• Fort Laramie

Pioneers followed the California, Oregon, and Mormon trails through Wyoming. They traveled the trails along the North Platte and Sweetwater rivers. After South Pass City, the trails headed in separate directions.

Pioneers carved their names on Independence Rock and Register Cliff. These were both located along the Oregon Trail.

Fort Laramie National Historic Site is near Fort Laramie. Soldiers here protected pioneers along the Oregon Trail and other westbound trails.

COLORADO

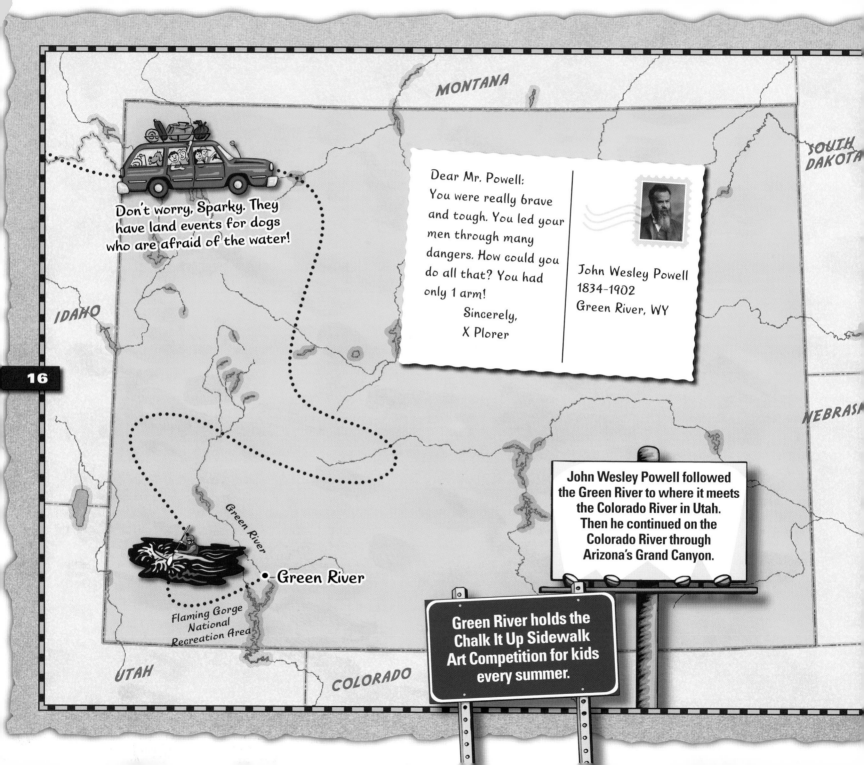

Don't worry, Sparky. They have land events for dogs who are afraid of the water!

Dear Mr. Powell:
You were really brave and tough. You led your men through many dangers. How could you do all that? You had only 1 arm!

Sincerely,
X Plorer

John Wesley Powell
1834-1902
Green River, WY

John Wesley Powell followed the Green River to where it meets the Colorado River in Utah. Then he continued on the Colorado River through Arizona's Grand Canyon.

Green River holds the Chalk It Up Sidewalk Art Competition for kids every summer.

Green River

Flaming Gorge National Recreation Area

MONTANA

SOUTH DAKOTA

IDAHO

NEBRASKA

UTAH

COLORADO

The Powell Plunge River Festival

Watch the duck race. See people do tricks in their **kayaks.** Or check out the dog contest. People throw sticks into the river. Their dogs jump in and fetch the sticks. Good doggies!

You're enjoying the Powell Plunge River Festival. It's held in Green River. Lots of people pass through this town. They're heading into Flaming Gorge. This deep canyon has colorful rock walls. The Green River runs through it.

John Wesley Powell explored this river in 1869. He began his journey in the town of Green River. It was called Green River City then. The river festival is named after him!

What a view! The Green River carved this canyon thousands of years ago.

Flaming Gorge National Recreation Area continues over Wyoming's border into Utah.

Wyoming's state motto is "Equal Rights."

18

Lawmakers are hard at work inside Wyoming's capitol.

See that statue in front of the capitol? It's Esther Hobart Morris. She made history in 1870. She became South Pass City's justice of the peace. That's a type of judge. Morris served for about eight months. No woman had ever held such a post before. The statue stands as a symbol of women's rights.

The capitol is Wyoming's state government building. The state government is divided into three branches. One branch makes state laws. Its members meet in the capitol. Another branch sees that laws are obeyed. The governor heads this branch. Judges make up the third branch. They decide whether laws have been broken.

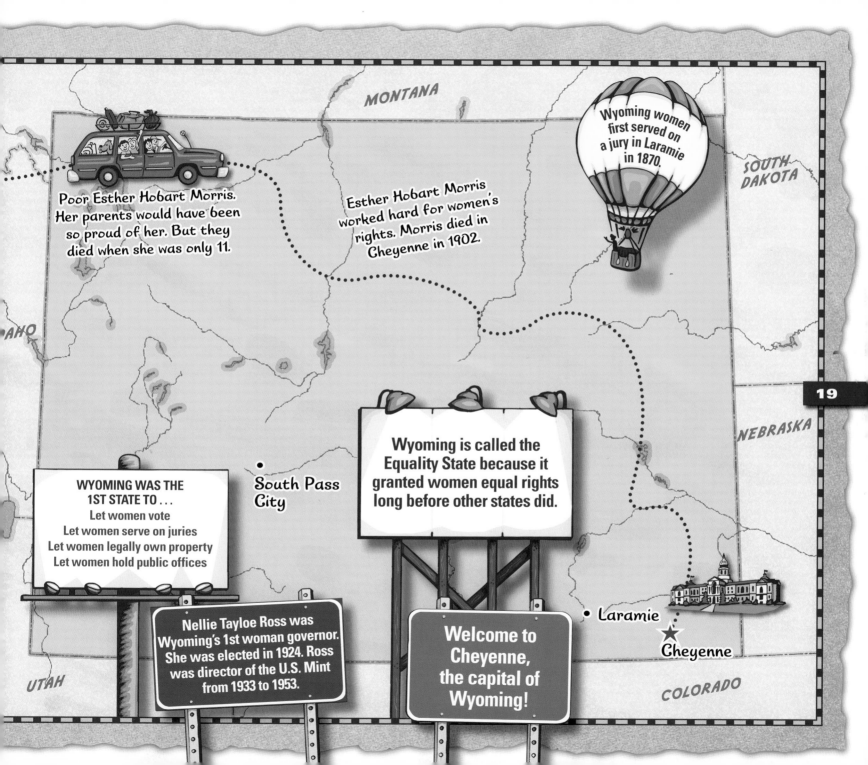

Poor Esther Hobart Morris. Her parents would have been so proud of her. But they died when she was only 11.

Esther Hobart Morris worked hard for women's rights. Morris died in Cheyenne in 1902.

MONTANA

SOUTH DAKOTA

Wyoming women first served on a jury in Laramie in 1870.

NEBRASKA

19

WYOMING WAS THE 1ST STATE TO . . .
Let women vote
Let women serve on juries
Let women legally own property
Let women hold public offices

• South Pass City

Wyoming is called the Equality State because it granted women equal rights long before other states did.

Nellie Tayloe Ross was Wyoming's 1st woman governor. She was elected in 1924. Ross was director of the U.S. Mint from 1933 to 1953.

Welcome to Cheyenne, the capital of Wyoming!

• Laramie

★ Cheyenne

UTAH

COLORADO

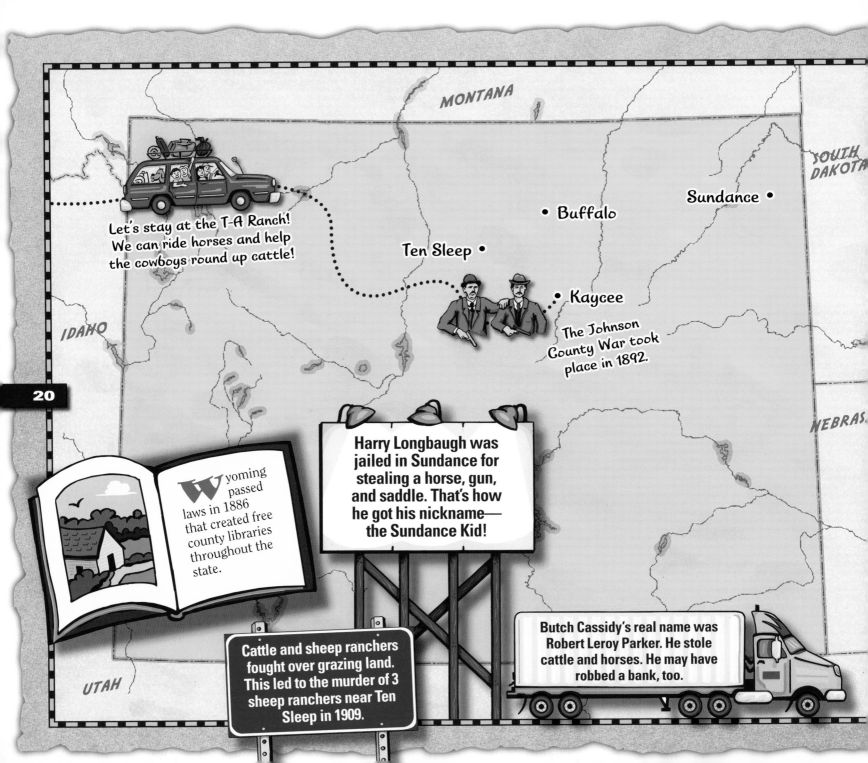

MONTANA

SOUTH DAKOTA

IDAHO

Let's stay at the T-A Ranch! We can ride horses and help the cowboys round up cattle!

Sundance •

• Buffalo

Ten Sleep •

• Kaycee

The Johnson County War took place in 1892.

NEBRAS.

Wyoming passed laws in 1886 that created free county libraries throughout the state.

Harry Longbaugh was jailed in Sundance for stealing a horse, gun, and saddle. That's how he got his nickname— the Sundance Kid!

Cattle and sheep ranchers fought over grazing land. This led to the murder of 3 sheep ranchers near Ten Sleep in 1909.

Butch Cassidy's real name was Robert Leroy Parker. He stole cattle and horses. He may have robbed a bank, too.

UTAH

Outlaws and Cattle Wars

Can you name some famous outlaws? How about Butch Cassidy and the Sundance Kid? They were bank robbers and horse thieves. They had a great hideout in Wyoming. It was called Hole-in-the-Wall!

Hole-in-the-Wall is a rocky canyon full of caves. You can visit this spot near Kaycee. You can even stay at nearby guest ranches. One is the famous T-A Ranch in Buffalo.

Some ranchers believed people were stealing their cattle. They decided to take the law into their own hands. They formed a group called the Invaders. Their purpose? To find the thieves and kill them! This was called the Johnson County War. The Invaders were finally captured at the T-A Ranch.

Want to see where famous outlaws hid? Check out Hole-in-the-Wall!

Wyoming was the 44th state to enter the Union. It joined on July 10, 1890.

Dude Ranching in Saratoga

Learn to care for a horse. Have a breakfast cookout around the campfire. Learn rope tricks from real cowboys. You're enjoying kids' programs at Brush Creek Ranch!

This is one of Wyoming's many dude ranches. *Dude* has a special meaning in the West. It's a city person unfamiliar with cowboy life. So dude ranches are for dudes!

Cattle ranching is Wyoming's biggest farm activity. Beef cattle are the most valuable farm products. Sheep and dairy cattle are important, too.

Most of Wyoming's farmland is naturally dry. But farmers use **irrigation** in their fields. Many farmers raise crops used as animal feed.

Round up some cattle at Brush Creek Ranch.

Only Texas and California raise more sheep than Wyoming.

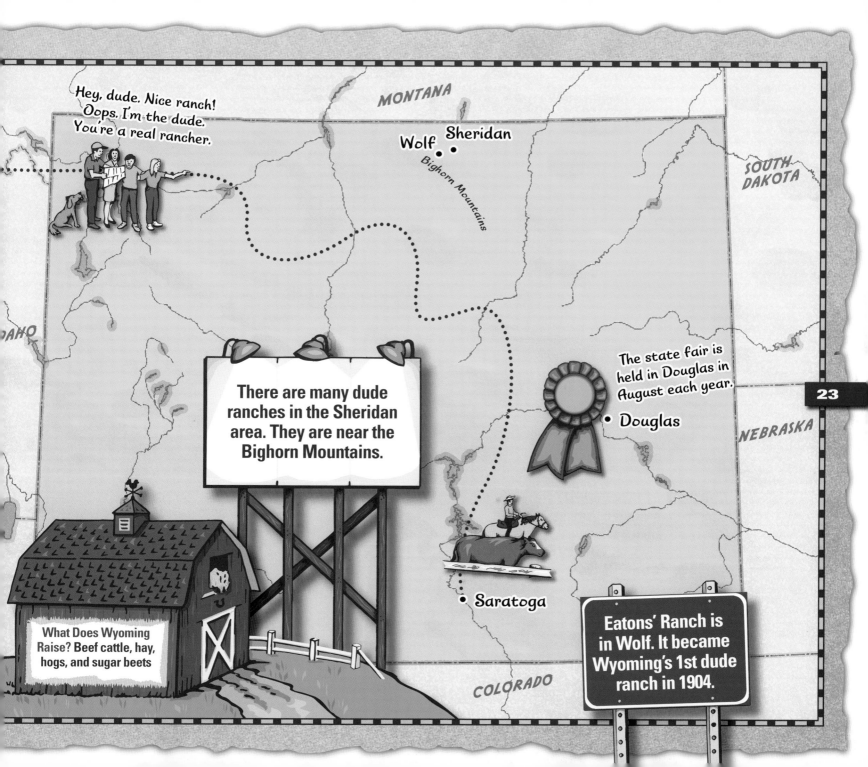

Hey, dude. Nice ranch!
Oops. I'm the dude.
You're a real rancher.

MONTANA

Wolf • Sheridan

Bighorn Mountains

SOUTH DAKOTA

IDAHO

There are many dude ranches in the Sheridan area. They are near the Bighorn Mountains.

The state fair is held in Douglas in August each year.

• Douglas

NEBRASKA

23

What Does Wyoming Raise? Beef cattle, hay, hogs, and sugar beets

• Saratoga

Eatons' Ranch is in Wolf. It became Wyoming's 1st dude ranch in 1904.

COLORADO

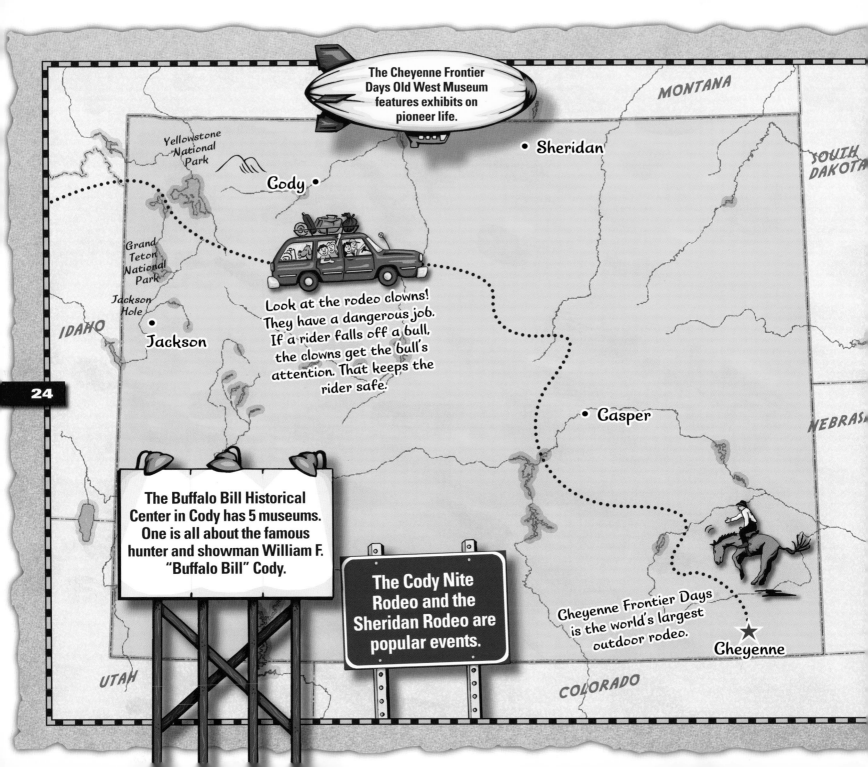

The Cheyenne Frontier Days Old West Museum features exhibits on pioneer life.

MONTANA

SOUTH DAKOTA

Yellowstone National Park

Cody

Sheridan

Grand Teton National Park

Jackson Hole

Jackson

IDAHO

Look at the rodeo clowns! They have a dangerous job. If a rider falls off a bull, the clowns get the bull's attention. That keeps the rider safe.

Casper

NEBRASKA

The Buffalo Bill Historical Center in Cody has 5 museums. One is all about the famous hunter and showman William F. "Buffalo Bill" Cody.

The Cody Nite Rodeo and the Sheridan Rodeo are popular events.

Cheyenne Frontier Days is the world's largest outdoor rodeo.

Cheyenne

UTAH

COLORADO

Cheyenne Frontier Days

Watch the cowboys and cowgirls. Some are roping bulls. Some are racing around barrels on fast horses. And some are riding bucking **broncos.** You're in Cheyenne for Frontier Days! It has one of the world's largest rodeos.

Rodeos are popular events in Wyoming. And no wonder. Real cowboys work on all those ranches!

Millions of visitors come to Wyoming every year. Many visit Yellowstone and Grand Teton national parks. They hike through the wilderness or watch animals. The mountains are great for climbing and snowmobiling, too. In winter, skiers head for the snowy slopes. Jackson Hole near Jackson is a favorite skiing spot.

This looks like a dangerous job. Watch real cowboys in action at Frontier Days.

Casper holds the Central Wyoming Fair and Rodeo every year.

Coal mining is important in Wyoming.
Visit a mine to see how it's done!

Laramie River Station

Tall smokestacks rise above the plains. You've reached the Laramie River Station! It's a big power plant near Wheatland. It burns coal to produce electricity. Step inside for a tour. You'll see its massive machines at work.

Wyoming has huge coal deposits. Many coal-burning power plants were built in the 1960s. Power plants can harm the **environment.** But workers at the Laramie River Station are careful. Equipment there helps protect the land, air, and water.

Wyoming produces more coal than any other state. It's rich in other minerals, too. One is trona. That's used in making glass, detergent, and paper. Another is bentonite. It's used to make paint, cosmetics, and crayons.

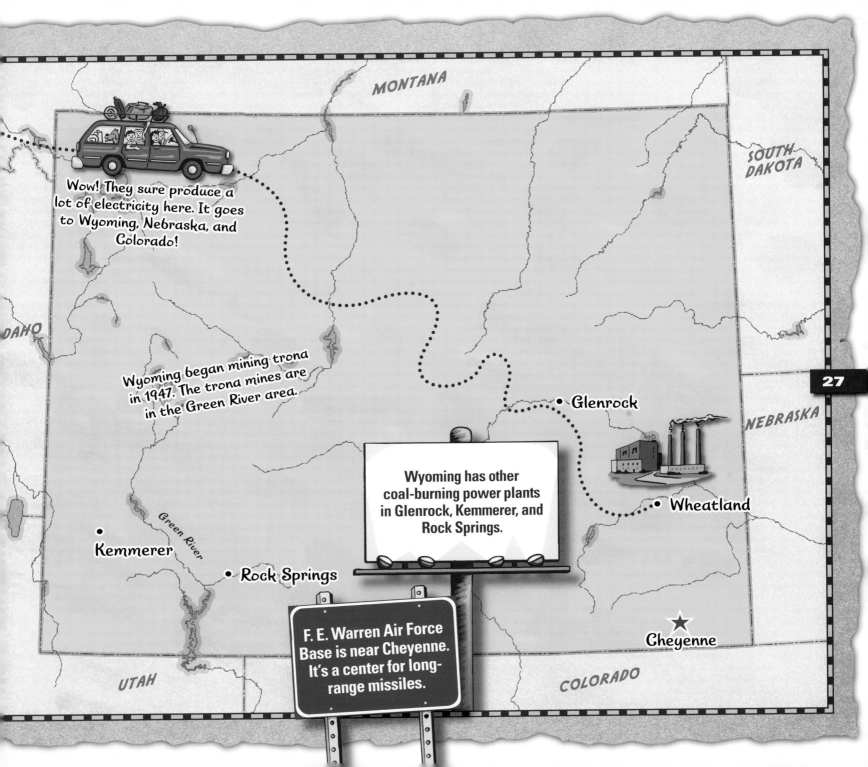

Wow! They sure produce a lot of electricity here. It goes to Wyoming, Nebraska, and Colorado!

Wyoming began mining trona in 1947. The trona mines are in the Green River area.

Wyoming has other coal-burning power plants in Glenrock, Kemmerer, and Rock Springs.

F. E. Warren Air Force Base is near Cheyenne. It's a center for long-range missiles.

MONTANA

SOUTH DAKOTA

IDAHO

NEBRASKA

Green River

Glenrock

Wheatland

Kemmerer

Rock Springs

Cheyenne

UTAH

COLORADO

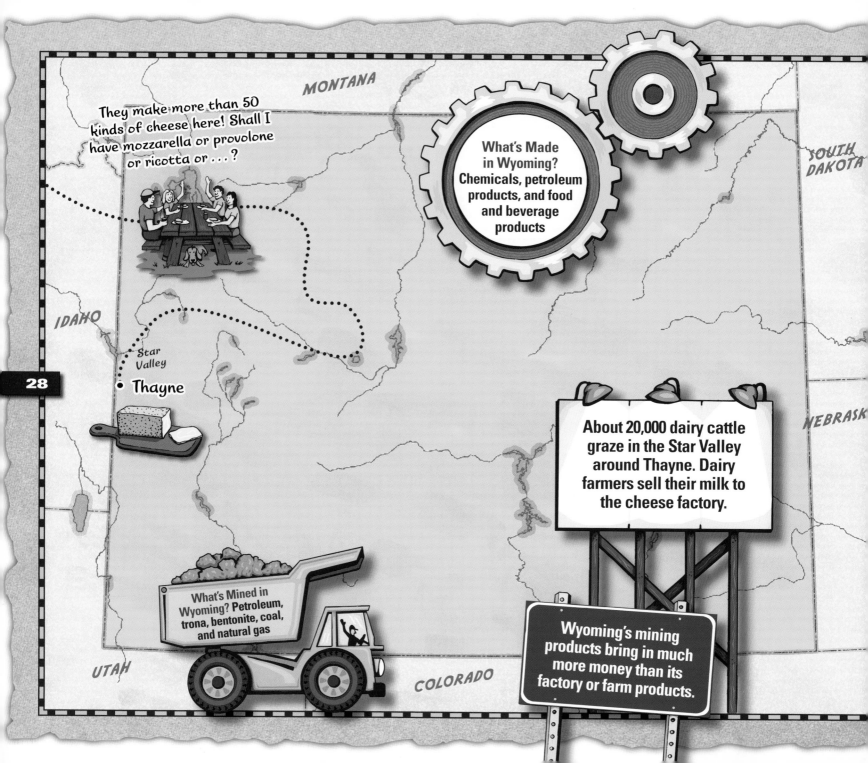

Star Valley Cheese in Thayne

Want a nice, gooey grilled cheese sandwich? Why not eat one at a cheese factory? Just stop by Star Valley Cheese in Thayne. You can watch people making cheese. Then you can try lots of free samples. And finish up with that grilled cheese sandwich!

Cheese is one of Wyoming's delicious food products. Others include butter, sugar, and soft drinks. But **chemicals** are the leading factory goods. Soda ash is the major chemical product. It's made from the mineral trona. Many factories process oil, too. They take impure materials out of the oil. The oil can then be used to make gasoline.

How is milk turned into cheese and curds? See for yourself at Star Valley Cheese!

Soda ash is also called sodium carbonate.

Gillette's Celtic Festival and Highland Games

Want to experience Celtic culture?
Just head to Gillette!

Almost 1 out of 5 people in Wyoming have roots in Scotland or Ireland.

Come to the Celtic Festival and Highland Games. People celebrate Scottish and Irish traditions here. You'll see activities you've never heard of before!

Many of the men are wearing kilts. Those are traditional plaid skirts. In one event, they toss heavy logs. Then they toss big bags of hay. Finally, there's a haggis-tossing event. Haggis is a Scottish food made with sheep stomachs!

Many **immigrants** moved into Wyoming. German people were the largest immigrant group. Others came from Norway and Sweden. Wyoming never got very crowded, though. It has the smallest population among all the states!

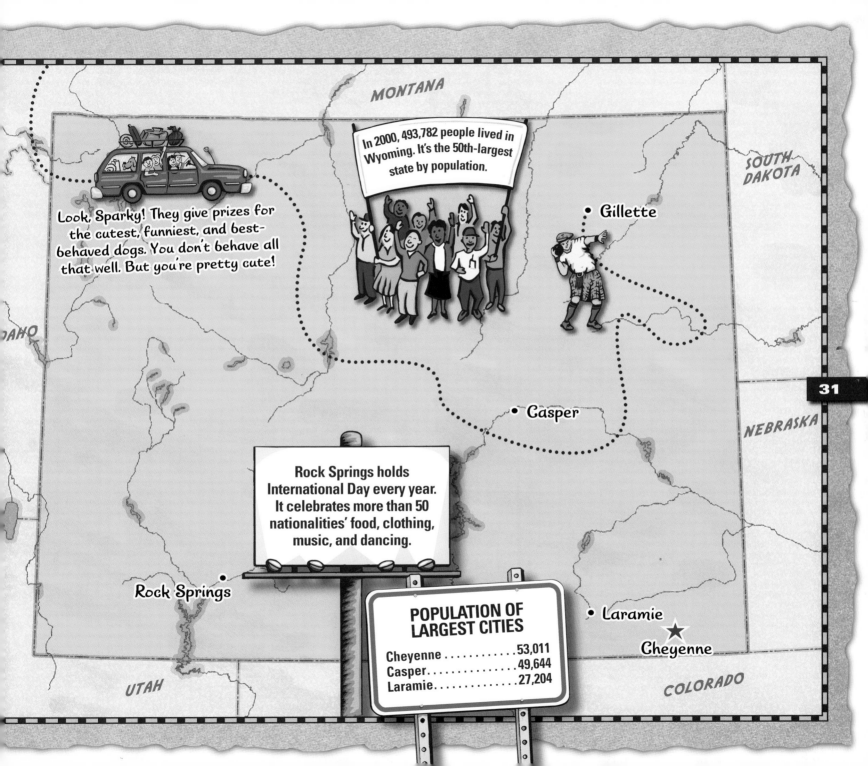

Look, Sparky! They give prizes for the cutest, funniest, and best-behaved dogs. You don't behave all that well. But you're pretty cute!

In 2000, 493,782 people lived in Wyoming. It's the 50th-largest state by population.

Rock Springs holds International Day every year. It celebrates more than 50 nationalities' food, clothing, music, and dancing.

POPULATION OF LARGEST CITIES

Cheyenne 53,011
Casper. 49,644
Laramie. 27,204

MONTANA
SOUTH DAKOTA
• Gillette
IDAHO
• Casper
NEBRASKA
Rock Springs
• Laramie
★ Cheyenne
UTAH
COLORADO

They give us digging tools.
We get a rock hammer, a
pick, and a little shovel. We
get a paintbrush, too. It's for
dusting dirt off the bones!

Thermopolis

Casper •

The University of
Wyoming Geological
Museum in Laramie has
lots of dinosaur exhibits.

You'll see many dinosaur
skeletons in the Tate
Geological Museum. It's at
Casper College in Casper.

• Laramie

MONTANA

SOUTH DAKOTA

IDAHO

NEBRAS

UTAH

COLORADO

Digging for Dinos in Thermopolis

Want to go digging for dinosaurs? Just drop by the Wyoming Dinosaur Center. It holds dino digs for kids and families. Real dinosaur scientists show you what to do.

Dinosaurs used to roam around here. Their remains are buried all over this area. Who knows? Maybe you'll find some bones!

Wander through the Dinosaur Center. It has life-size dinosaur models. You'll be amazed at how big these creatures were! You can watch scientists at work there, too. They're cleaning **fossils** and studying bones. Would you like to be a dinosaur scientist? You could make an exciting discovery!

Watch out for the *Triceratops*! You'll see plenty of fossils in Thermopolis!

About 50 different types of dinosaurs have been found in Wyoming.

Do you write notes to your friends? Wyoming pioneers did at Independence Rock!

Independence Rock

Pioneers knew Independence Rock well. It's right by the Sweetwater River. They could see the rock from far away. Some said it looked like an upside-down bowl. Others said it was like a giant turtle or whale.

Independence Rock was actually like a big bulletin board. Pioneers carved or painted their names on it. Some carved messages for friends who were coming later. It was exciting to find a friend's note!

Want to climb to the top of the rock? You'll see hundreds of names up there. It's fun to read the messages!

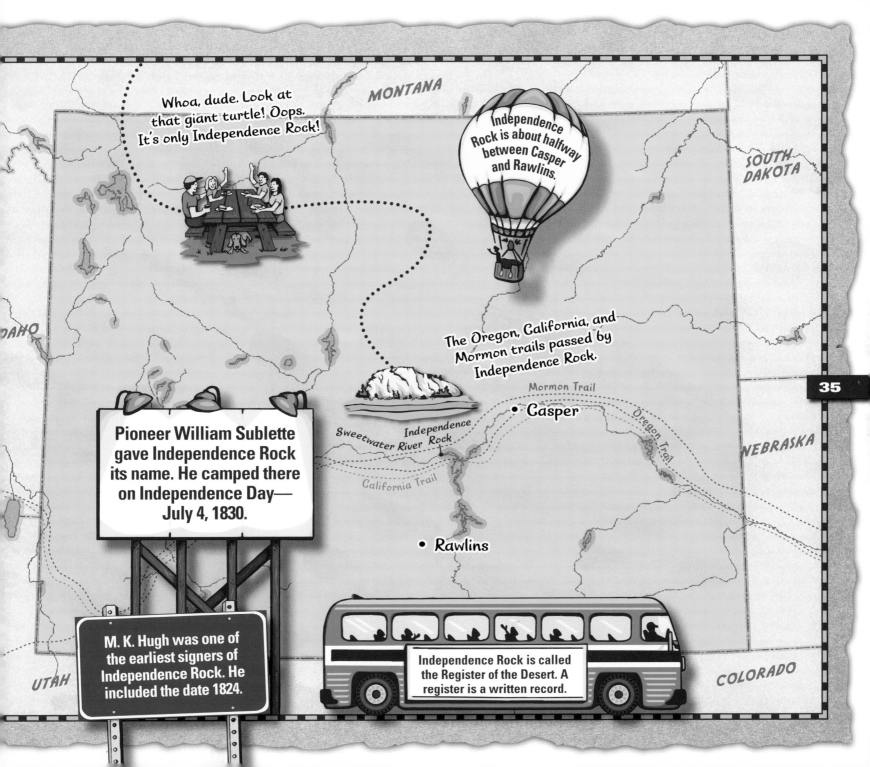

Whoa, dude. Look at that giant turtle! Oops. It's only Independence Rock!

MONTANA

SOUTH DAKOTA

Independence Rock is about halfway between Casper and Rawlins.

IDAHO

The Oregon, California, and Mormon trails passed by Independence Rock.

35

Mormon Trail

• Casper

Oregon Trail

Sweetwater River

Independence Rock

NEBRASKA

California Trail

Pioneer William Sublette gave Independence Rock its name. He camped there on Independence Day— July 4, 1830.

• Rawlins

M. K. Hugh was one of the earliest signers of Independence Rock. He included the date 1824.

Independence Rock is called the Register of the Desert. A register is a written record.

UTAH

COLORADO

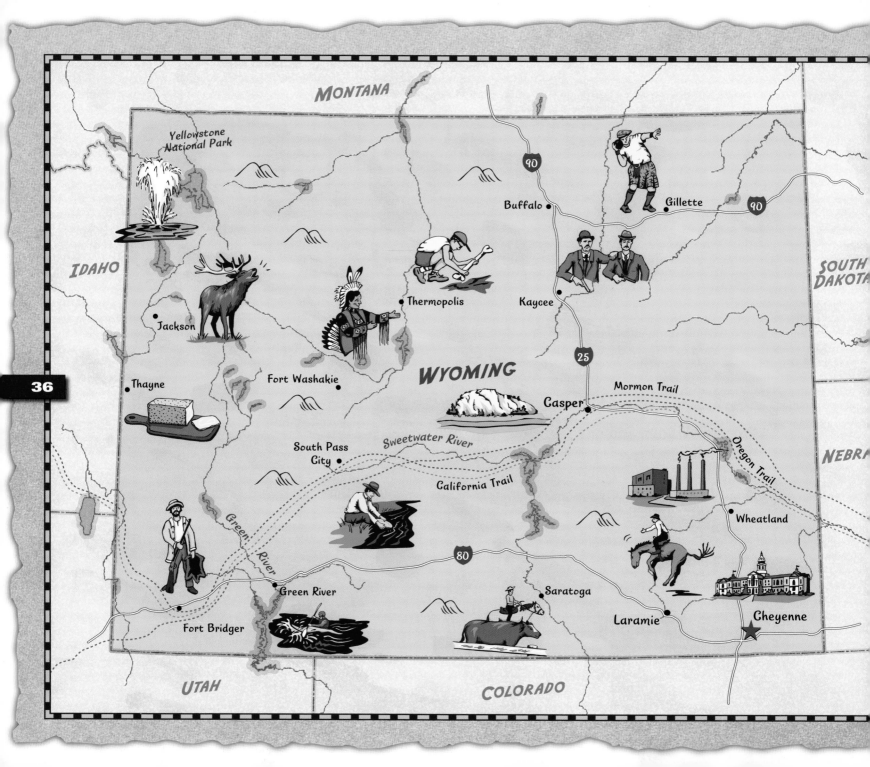

MONTANA

Yellowstone
National Park

IDAHO

Jackson

Fort Washakie

WYOMING

Thermopolis

Buffalo

90

Gillette

90

Kaycee

SOUTH
DAKOTA

Thayne

25

Casper

Mormon Trail

South Pass
City

Sweetwater River

California Trail

Oregon Trail

NEBRA

Green River

Wheatland

80

Saratoga

Fort Bridger

Green River

Laramie

Cheyenne

UTAH

COLORADO

OUR TRIP

We visited many amazing places on our trip! We also met a lot of interesting people along the way. Look at the map on the left. Use your finger to trace all the places we have been.

How often does Old Faithful erupt? See page 7 for the answer.

When do elk shed their antlers? See page 9 for the answer.

What are stick games? See page 11 for the answer.

What trails did pioneers follow through Wyoming? See page 15 for the answer.

Where is the Chalk It Up Sidewalk Art Competition held? See page 16 for the answer.

Why is Wyoming called the Equality State? See page 19 for the answer.

When did Wyoming begin mining trona? See page 27 for the answer.

How many types of dinosaurs have been found in Wyoming? See page 33 for the answer.

That was a great trip! We have traveled all over Wyoming! There are a few places that we didn't have time for, though. Next time, we plan to visit the Ames Pyramid in Laramie. The pyramid was built to honor the Ames brothers. They manufactured shovels in the 1800s. Their shovels were used to dig the transcontinental railroad.

More Places to Visit in Wyoming

WORDS TO KNOW

broncos (BRAWN-koz) wild or partly tamed horses or ponies

chemicals (KEM-uh-kuhlz) substances made by processing minerals in various ways

culture (KUL-chur) a group of people's customs, beliefs, and way of life

endangered (in-DAYN-jurd) in danger of dying off

environment (en-VYE-run-muhnt) natural surroundings, such as air, water, and soil

fossils (FOSS-uhlz) remains or prints of animals or plants left in stone

geology (jee-OL-uh-jee) the study of rocks

geysers (GUY-zurz) underground springs that spray out hot water and steam

immigrants (IM-uh-gruhnts) people who move to another country

irrigation (ihr-uh-GAY-shuhn) a method of bringing water to fields through ditches or pipes

kayaks (KIE-acks) boats that are covered or closed, with a hole for the boater's body

mudpots (MUD-pots) boiling pools of acid, clay, and hot water

rendezvous (RON-day-voo) French word that means "meeting"

reservation (rez-ur-VAY-shuhn) land set aside for use by American Indians

traditional (truh-DISH-uh-nul) following long-held customs

Wyoming covers 97,100 square miles (251,489 sq km). It's the 9th-largest state in size.

STATE SYMBOLS

State bird: Western meadowlark

State dinosaur: *Triceratops*

State fish: Cutthroat trout

State flower: Indian paintbrush

State fossil: Knightia

State gemstone: Jade

State mammal: American bison (buffalo)

State reptile: Horned toad

State sport: Rodeo

State tree: Plains cottonwood

State flag

State seal

STATE SONG

"Wyoming"

Words by C. E. Winter, music by G. E. Knapp

In the far and mighty West,
Where the crimson sun seeks rest,
There's a growing splendid State
that lies above,
On the breast of this great land;
Where the massive Rockies stand,
There's Wyoming young and strong,
the State I love!

Chorus:
Wyoming, Wyoming! Land of the
sunlight clear!
Wyoming, Wyoming! Land that we
hold so dear!
Wyoming, Wyoming! Precious art
thou and thine!
Wyoming, Wyoming! Beloved State
of mine!

In the flowers wild and sweet,
Colors rare and perfumes meet;
There's the columbine so pure, the
daisy too,
Wild the rose and red it springs,
White the button and its rings,
Thou art loyal for they're red and
white and blue.

(Chorus)

Where thy peaks with crowned
head,
Rising till the sky they wed,
Sit like snow queens ruling wood
and stream and plain;
'Neath thy granite bases deep,
'Neath thy bosom's broadened
sweep,
Lie the riches that have gained and
brought thee fame.

(Chorus)

Other treasures thou dost hold,
Men and women thou dost mould,
True and earnest are the lives that
thou dost raise,
Strengthen thy children though dost
teach,
Nature's truth thou givest to each,
Free and noble are thy workings and
thy ways.

(Chorus)

In the nation's banner free
There's one star that has for me
A radiance pure and splendor like
the sun;
Mine it is, Wyoming's star,
Home it leads me near or far;
O Wyoming! All my heart and love
you've won!

FAMOUS PEOPLE

Bridger, James (1804–1881), pioneer and mountain man

Cheney, Dick (1941–), vice president under President George W. Bush

Cody, William "Buffalo Bill" (1846–1917), scout and showman

Colter, John (ca. 1775–1813), explorer

Crazy Horse (ca. 1842–1877), American Indian warrior

Dowler, Boyd (1937–), football player

Downey, June Etta (1875–1932), educator and psychologist

Gardner, Rulon (1971–), athlete and Olympic medalist

Jackson, Harry (1924–), artist

Jewell, Isabel (1907–1972), actor

MacLachlan, Patricia (1938–), children's author

Molesworth, Thomas (1890–1977), furniture maker

Morris, Esther Hobart (1814–1902), women's rights pioneer

Pollock, Jackson (1912–1956), artist

Ross, Nellie Tayloe (1876–1977), 1st woman governor in the United States

Simpson, Alan (1931–), U.S. senator

Smith, Jedediah (1799–1831), fur trader and explorer

Swallow, Alan (1915–1966), author and publisher

Washakie (ca. 1798–1900), American Indian leader

TO FIND OUT MORE

At the Library

Gagliano, Eugene, and Susan Guy (illustrator). *C Is for Cowboy: A Wyoming Alphabet.* Chelsea, Mich.: Sleeping Bear Press, 2003.

Hanson-Harding, Alexandra. *Wyoming.* New York: Children's Press, 2003.

MacLachlan, Patricia, and Barry Moser. *What You Know First.* New York: HarperCollins Publishers, 1995.

St. George, Judith. *Crazy Horse.* New York: Putnam's, 1994.

On the Web

Visit our home page for lots of links about Wyoming: *http://www.childsworld.com/links*

Note to Parents, Teachers, and Librarians: We routinely verify our Web links to make sure they are safe, active sites—so encourage your readers to check them out!

Places to Visit or Contact

Wyoming Division of Travel and Tourism
I-25 at College Drive
Cheyenne, WY 82002
307/777-7777
For more information about traveling in Wyoming

Wyoming State Museum
Barrett Building
2301 Central Avenue
Cheyenne, WY 82002
307/777-7022
For more information about the history of Wyoming

INDEX

Bye, Equality State. We had a great time. We'll come back soon!